Gender Artist

For my only child.
You are Everyman. Everywoman is you.
All pieces of the puzzle called creation.
I launched you. I'm still trembling.

Cover illustration: Istry Istry

Cover and page design by Anna Myers Sabatini

ISBN: 978-1-7328414-8-2

Library of Congress Control Number: 2021903596

Schwartz, Lee (Lee A.).
Gender artist : a mother's poems about raising a queer child in a
straight world / Lee A. Schwartz.
Housatonic, Massachusetts : Green Fire Press, [2021].
76 pages
9781732841482
1. Transgender children — Poetry.
PS3619.C459 G46 2021
811.54 (23 ed.)

Green
Fire
Press

Green Fire Press
PO Box 377 Housatonic MA 01236

Gender Artist

*A mother's poems about raising a queer child
in a straight world*

Lee Schwartz

GREEN FIRE PRESS | HOUSATONIC, MASSACHUSETTS

Author's Note

I wrote these poems over a period of 15 years, as I observed my five-year-old daughter changing to my 20-year old trans-masculine child. In the initial poems presented here, "she" is still "daughter." Then there is a morphing of the male rising, as I transition to his new preferred pronoun. Some names have been changed to protect privacy.

Contents

Gender Artist

Mother Midnight

It wasn't when you told me you were gay,

hey, a mother knew that was coming,

my girl playing Dungeons and Dragons,

swinging against the ribbon of girldom.

But when you started wearing men's underwear,

entering men's rooms, changed your name,

told me at age twenty: I feel more like a man,

than a woman — sometimes neither;

That's when I ran to the poem,

dragged myself on my knees before the page,

confessed my wildest thoughts, my rage, my regrets

upon the blank altar in the dark of mother midnight.

I asked for understanding. To unravel the mystery—

what was happening to my child?

I gave everything to the poem.

My blood smeared the page, my bones rattled the desk.

Would my child be safe, find love? Would he jump down a well

to be lost forever?

I embraced the page as an island to love my child

in whatever form he appears. I want to be close, to hear his voice,

to share his life as the layers of his self morph.

I write of sloughing away the softness, fighting the biology of
    destiny, roaring his fiery heart;

my child inside-outing his femaleness, dumpster diving,

embracing his man stride, his new "male privilege."

Everything about you is a poem.

I can't stop writing your treatise of becoming,

exalting the language of queerdom.

I must be as brave as you, and on the page I can be,

risking all to be one, within and without.

I see you as whole now, I write you as whole now,

I love you as whole now.

I ask myself, who would do this if not to save one's life?

You, through the sacred ground of trans living, and me,

through the act of scribbling my soul onto an accepting paper god.

When Did I Know?

An iconoclast at five,

you stopped wearing pink,

ripped the bows out,

pants replaced thumb sucking for comfort.

At ten, it was plaid shirts, jeans and high tops

from the boys' department.

The saleslady said,

"Your son will love these."

Other girls were playing pretty,

glitter garb and spikey heels,

as you sped across ice rinks

in sweaty face mask and pads

Denying breasts and period blood,

slipping gold on upper ear,

an alchemy no scientist can factor,

breaking he/she spines on books.

Chasing Freud, frauds and circus clowns,

my child rewriting history.

A mother knows, in the cavern of the bones,

who you are and who you love.

Restless is your hero's voice

as you write of a gay Romeo

climbing up gender's balcony

to announce your troth.

Was this your white plume?

I thought so...

when you brought a girl home,

to the closed tower of your room.

Just shy of sixteen, trembling, you face me,

Mom, I need to tell you something

you already know—

certain in your tee shirt

and onion smell of separation.

Sawing a Lady in Half

Second grade you chose to dress

as Houdini on "Who Am I?" day—

black suit, top hat, white gloves.

The other girls were stacked to the stars

on Jackie O, flappers and saints,

ladies with flounces, lipstick and bling.

You, a short man who saws ladies in half,

laying them down on a hard black table,

steel blade to their crinolined ribs.

The tuxedo charmer adjusts his cuffs,

the girl in you vanishes,

the Russian, Jewish trickster appears,

my son, on stage.

Doves fly, girls swoon,

my child attempting the greatest illusion,

out of trunks, out of chains, flesh set free.

Behind what trap door is she hiding?

Under what floor board, silent and frozen?

The Great Magician bows, owning the stage.

Pony tail tucked under tall hat,

swirling his red silk-lined cape,

he swaggers, strutting his power to transform.

The hockey mask and baseball cleats came later,

props and costumes for a "real" man,

the color of mud, jerseys and generals.

A man who performs alchemy,

conjures Eve back into Adam's rib:

my daughter, the escape artist.

A Fireman Enters, 2001

On your eleventh Halloween you crossed

the sexual divide by posing as a 9/11 fireman.

You stomped in and all the princesses

and witches clapped and hooted.

Our hero in black plastic helmet,

seltzer bottles strapped on back,

pretend ax, oversize boots,

ready to snuff out flames and false facades.

You are the one we want,

a hero to sweep us up and hold fast,

not some rouged-up vampet

in high heels and press-on nails.

You, daughter, fierce and fiery,

standing tall in the heat of giggles

in your Don Quixote asbestos,

fanning this fanfare.

It's all smoke and party pants

but they want to believe

in your muscles, heart and guts,

clearing a path through the orange haze.

When the party's over,

will they still shout and cheer

at the wonder of who you are:

a house on fire in sparks and overalls?

At Eleven and a Half

Your breasts, like mine at puberty,

skin rising out of the chest plate,

a magic trick, balls in the air,

English tea cups on saucers.

Fifties bumper bombers,

air trembling between bra and tee,

the raw mystery of you,

in circus pants and spongy sneakers that say *cool*.

Angel and man in tow,

opulent as a continental shelf,

you will squeeze the next generation

between your hockey thighs.

You are me and my mother before,

all women in motion, a lullaby in work boots,

there is no stopping the crests, the moons,

the danger, rising up to declare itself.

Sleeping lioness, sharpen your claws,

soon young men will circle to taste

your creamy orbs,

your chest a cheeseburger deluxe.

My Daughter Wears Men's Underwear

Coxcombing the crotch and weave,

my daughter wears men's underwear

over the ravine of her sex.

Trekking out to pitcher's plate,

leaving her cello on the floor

next to her art stuff,

My daughter betrays lip gloss,

muscles like meat loaf,

hairy legs and hi tops on the mound.

Men's blue jeans sluice hipbone,

a ridge of guy regalia

circling her pelvis, warming her ass.

Male flag colors of gray and blue,

a shock of red rising like toast

at the lip of the crossroads.

Pulling them up over painted piglet toes,

stepping into the crosshatches of maledom,

walking out of her sex like James Dean,

Wounded for wanting

to rewrite the script —

to kiss a guy in the back seat of his coupe.

I grieve for the little girl lost,

no Madeline dresses with fat bows,

no tea parties with pinkies raised.

I'm not ready to give up

my pink pearl '50s fantasy of you,

painted on velvet awaiting your prince.

Maybe this is better —

you are your own prince in Jockeys,

kicking up dust, cursing like a king.

Chick Magnet

When your back is facing me

I don't know if it's you or daddy —

there's the man in you.

Facing me now, feet akimbo,

one lip goes up, like Elvis,

poised for a larger arena.

The man in you breaking free,

defying the mango smoothie voice,

scraggly-ass hair under hip hop hat,

A total force-of-nature chick magnet.

You adore tiny women, nosegays of girls,

bird bones, small wrists and fingers,

jewels you hold in your hand, in the curl of your lap.

The pixie fragile femmes

I always longed to be, the ones boys asked to dance

and made out with behind the gym.

Never chosen to play the girl —

towering, baling wire and acne,

waiting years to claim my guiles,

to coax heat in a man.

Is this what I see when I look at you, daughter:

the frozen pelvis,

the locked breasts;

the man in me?

Big-boned and square-jawed,

my frame, my duality,

is this your inheritance?

Unicorn and Amazon wrestle to claim you.

At eighteen you let yourself be drawn

by the silent pull of a tiny, shiny nose ring.

When Did You Decide to be Straight?

My daughter is gay,

A sapphist, dyke, gender bender,

that's right – say it with me:

L-E-S-B-I-A-N

How could you not love her

standing over the stove making red velvet cake?

Came out at fifteen,

lion heart purring for a girl

with a diamond in her nose.

Skinny-dipped the Green River.

How could you not love her,

riding gender like a seahorse?

She loves women…she's into the Goddess.

She can't help it, nobody can.

When did you decide to be straight?

The pull, a raft down a Florida inlet of mangroves,

the cream at the center of orchids,

tangled by roots and wetness and mystery

into someone's pants and body hair,

the slippery slime of the peeping crocodile

getting tangled in a Lady's Slipper.

At twelve, I stood by the school bus,

boys parading past me, sneakers flying

and the smell—the rough boy smell

of contact sports and locker room tongue.

I dreamed of kissing those salty boys…

leaning to lick the sweat off their necks.

Please don't take my child in some alley,

tearing off her fronds and petals,

to see what nature is this rose.

Let her live in her half-Venus bloom.

Every act of becoming is a celebration.

Talking Turkey

I took the dross

of your hair from the garbage

on Thanksgiving, as you stomped:

THIS SUCKS, I DON'T WANT

TO BE HERE, YOU SMOTHER ME

WITH THIS PERFECT LOVE OF AN

ONLY CHILD, GIVING ME WHAT

I NEED BEFORE I KNOW I NEED IT,

I CAN'T SEE YOU ANYMORE ON

THANKSGIVING, IT'S AN IMPERIALIST,

COLONIALIST HOLIDAY THAT IS ABOUT

POWER OVER INDIGENOUS PEOPLE.

I cupped your snippings,

like Jesus in the crèche,

a souvenir of the girl I lost

before you became a man.

Standing before the mirror

shearing off lakes, canyons, and mountain ranges,

home to grizzlies, wolves, and packs of coyotes,

you drift off to a new tribe,

far from our Patriarchal Oppression,

your stallion hair, coarse and dark,

thick and flossy, bossy and untamed.

Pushing me away so you won't need me,

leaving me in the kitchen

while you relish the utopia of anger,

your mane is now a vast eco-system

of grasses I will never brush or snuggle.

Did Samson's mother keep his hair, too,

hidden under the dirt of her tent,

knowing it was not the source of his strength

but rather a flag he waved, a cloud, a blanket

to put his rivals and lovers off the scent?

Gay Sheep

There's a lab off the Pacific Highway

where they snare gay sheep to turn them straight.

No more woolly love come loping

by the top of the hill.

Replant fences, implant desire,

plump up thighs for slaughter chops.

Estrogen in a cold needle,

midwifing the sheepish natural order.

Playing God in the garden

to grow the market share,

hens on a timer,

salmon lost their way.

Tinkering with nature's Apps,

creating dwarf melons, mating grapes,

planet in a bottle,

nitrates in my d-o-n-u-t.

Grow me good will

while we go sheep shopping at the Gap,

don't tell me who to love,

whose name hovers in the hem of my tongue.

And the sheep with the coarse and wiry coat?

Would we prefer sleek and glossy?

What about seeing-eye cats? Faster turtles?

Deer that don't stop in the headlights?

You go down that long Pacific highway

and build a Sparta to keep up with the trends.

See if you can weed out the gene that pulls the trigger,

rapes women, and votes Republican.

Moon Roof

Mowing down the woman rising

a flower box

a frontier

a landing strip

no radar to bring you in

my kid's head shaved and shaggy,

a non-conforming doo roof.

Your queer cut reveals your shrimp-like ears

solid Carthaginian neck

this purple swirl says

queer in your face

in your space.

The ripples in the scalp trumpet

walking into public rest rooms

men's wear departments

Celtic dance contests

yurts, trailer parks

Dairy Queens —

They look… they stare:

Wonder if your mother knows

                          what's in your pants, boy.

What side of the garden do you grow?

This hair-raising is all about

passing strange,
    stepping through the looking glass

leaving biology
                    in the dust,

the fluid pleasure

of gender betrayal.

Passage du Rites

You appear, daughter, at my door

with a silver ball embedded in your

chin, closer to your lower lip,

androgyny's savage new portal.

I calmly assess the amulet

as you offer to make eggs,

Globus as the pleasure dome

heralding your late adolescence.

A lost comet come home,

irritating flesh, pleasure/pain,

impaling gum, sinews, tributaries,

screwed through to the inner fire.

When you kiss

the song of Circe calls,

wet lips and stiletto tongues,

a silver mine spilling sparks.

This shiny globe

reflects all that stands before it,

images of us gawking,

taking in your mannish form.

Dylan hair,

Chaplin suspenders,

squared off hips,

a whole universe of love and betrayal.

You serve the eggs garnished with cheese,

cumin and hot sauce,

hot sauce on everything,

a fire eater downing a poker.

Between the Cars

Low riders, fuzz on face,

jump off lifeguard chair into blue,

zipped inside a female body,

strutting turf like a man.

Binding milkweed breasts,

peeling them off like an orange,

real man pecs under plaid shirt,

chandelier hanging from one ear.

You see *h/im* sitting across

on the L train

and you stare,

eyeballing in slow mo.

Close enough to touch,

Rodin hairy legs,

silver ball hovers by,

smooth-as-lake lips.

Rolled up sleeves, revved up shoes,

baby pink cheek,

eye contact becomes a risk,

no F or M box signal.

Hoisting fluidity like a flag,

spilling out into the car,

the tiny hairs on neck

invite your turn-on.

Ears plug into dancemelt,

the master of riddles shuts eyes,

the aisle a river of doubt,

a game of chess — your move.

Beer bottles roll

toward Brooklyn,

the train rocks a steady

boy-girl, boy-girl, boy-girl.

Gender Artist

A human wind turbine,

inside outing fe/male to breathe h/s self,

living in her manskin, her rough hair, cut-offs,

to drink in all the voices and songs and forge

hisself as an amalgam of the best elements.

The flints and fires, irons and steel,

the baser metals that bond and heal,

up from the earth, neither sex applies,

fire heart to the wheel,

legs astride, stomping out binary idols.

Lightning Bug

You, my child, have lessons to teach about

saving the earth.

There is no sitting still,

there's work to be done.

I don't know how you got this light,

this beacon into the future that will

harness the earth and give folks a purpose.

I remember when I let you run to Hebrew School,

on your own, down the block—

your purple book bag jangling

behind you, keychains with silly

bugs and tiny characters jumping

and cheering you on to freedom

from mom,

freedom to go to the four points

of the earth and discover

your mantra.

You, a teacher like me,

but with the whole world as your

classroom, growing what is eternal

and green,

spreading news on fracking,

farming, Palestine, justice,

what it takes to grind and push,

shovel change for the masses

yearning to breathe free.

I birthed you, and you took off,

leaving me alone in the wonderment.

I want to feel the warmth of your light,

the flutter of your touch,

but you push me away, choosing

to give your love to strangers,

to those with no history of your trials,

how you came to understand that

you are *in-between*,

not she or he

but all of it:

The period blood and the

breaking of a chicken's neck,

harnessing the sun and tying a bow tie,

sweet and sassy, the dirt of farming,

the sweat of preaching, raising the breath

of blowing the shofar to the community.

You deny me the pride of knowing you

and showing you off to my circle.

You, a lightning bug to all the world,

sit in darkness at my door,

no signal of life for me,

the one who washed your hands off

after we built sand castles

by the rising tide.

Now you build nations, and choose to love

others who build dreams,

as I had for you.

War Chest

Casting your womanhood into the galaxy,

two moons sent off,

A blank canvas now facing us,

a flatland of masculinity,

Taut circumference of rings

with no planets, no stars, only the plains

Of your new gender, out in tight tee,

the centers of your nipples demure, tiny buds.

This your declaration:

to turn your back on destiny.

Sever the Queen Anne lace, the creamy cupcakes,

set out fresh daily to announce Woman,

Discarded remnants of sex's betrayal,

milky and warm, inflamed to attract,

Now there is a clearing, a hothouse leveled,

going on unto eternity,

A highway of ribbons and medals,

proudly displayed as your war chest, your coat of arms,

Won bravely in a war against nature, fighting the biology

that crowned you, cutting away the softness,

To be the hard shell, the wall of man,

a new mountain on the map of possibilities,

54

A sacred ground of trans-making man, the journey

toward which everything flows, like water through rocks.

You've Got (fe)Male

I am the blurred body of the future,
  the slow sloughing away of the line

that puts bodies in boxes,

a new model bio-fitted

to yield and grind,

flex or flax,

a hybrid of

the gender revolution.

Bliss and balls,

transreal zeitgeist,

best the two-legged beast

has to offer:

rational and teary,

flirty and flinty,

sneaker propelled.

Whatever I need to be

in any board room or forest,

equipped to deal and roll,

respire and respond,

trans driven / green living

hemp refining / tea imbibing

dumpster diving / pleasure wiring

without glory, caution or fences,

loving and performing universal personhood.

A Body to Die For

Oh brave new world

out of ribs to woman,

out of steroids to man,

Herculean love seat of our time.

Risking all to be one

within and without,

congruent in skin and sinew,

retro-fitted to avoid suicide.

For females: intramuscular vials,

two hundred mg of Depo-T,

causing a neo-teen outbreak

of crater moon acne and swell.

Blockers dam female menses,

pecs, abs and beard sprout,

angel's soprano song trained

into bellows of bats on barstools.

For males: chest implants, estrogen,

remove torso hair, a good runway

and voice therapist, wigs, make up,

Adam's apples shaved.

If resources and desire permit,

genital reassignment,

phalloplasty (create penis)

or vaginoplasty (design vagina).

To remove one's facial hair follicles,

one by one, to invert one's penis to a nosegay,

to smash and build cheek bones and jaws,

who would do this if not to save one's life?

Tech Mush

Now and then I get a text, a peep, a postcard.

You are 24 and live far away,

I fear you do not care or think about me in the old

symbiotic way of mother–child rock-a-bye baby.

Maybe now that I am in Oaxaca,

three thousand, thirty-eight miles away, you dare

to get close in a text.

Mini missive sugar darts:

Miss you, mom. Have a great time, mom,

Love you Mama Bear, if you need me, I'm your guy.

And it's so hard, when you are this effusive and velvety

not to think of you as *my daughter.*

I know I have strict instructions to call you by

the male pronoun,

and when you are a jerk and a bully, it's easy.

But when you are pink kisses

wrapped in tulle—it is the girl in you I feel,

the sweet, languorous voice that never changed,

that opted out

of hormone therapy.

.

So you are *my in-between kid* —neither here nor there,

him or her

an hourglass with the sugar flowing inside to the bottom

which becomes the top,

which becomes the bottom....

64

Changed name, cropped hair, breasts gone, blue fingernails—

I guess I'll never stop grieving, even as I fight for your rights

in the halls and streets of the world.

I love you in your men's underwear,

but I gave birth to a girl, and I miss her when you send me

these texts,

so girly,

not like you are in my face, raging at me like my psycho father,

accusing me of being a

BOURGEOIS OPPRESSIVE CAPITALIST SELFISH PRICK ASSHOLE

while you parade the idyllic privilege

of being my white male child.

So let me sop up the few drops of girly tech mush.

Let me let you love me for a precious few

fluid seconds,

before you return to the rooted and heady place of transman.

There They Lie

In the night table drawer
               cool, jumbled tiles
         piled on top
              of each other,

the A, the fat D, the proud first letter M
                       and the question Y.

A little bracelet you made at five or six,

stringing the black shoe lace through the white

stones with the hole in the middle of each block,

the black letter on all four sides,

so no matter how they fell, it was always

MANDY MANDY MANDY MANDY

And it was,

until

at twenty or twenty-one,

you dropped the M and announced you were now

ANDY all the time, ANDY CHARLES to be exact,

opera tenor hair climbing out of red hot beanie,

daddy's shirt, hands in pockets, sitting

legs astride over fluorescent hi-tops.

Mandy is gone and my child is a man.

Except for this little musty space in the bedside drawer

where your name lives on.

I like seeing the smooth, tooth-like letters

as I reach in to get a bookmark
                              or a nail clipper,
        your name, as ordinary
                         as the everyday thing I reach for,

as holy as the name I cry out in the night.

ABOUT THE AUTHOR

Born in Brooklyn, Lee Schwartz is a lifelong New Yorker. She graduated with advanced degrees from New York University and never left Greenwich Village, inspired by the surroundings and writers who lived there. She studied with Sharon Olds; Frida Kahlo is another mentor. Her work has been published in the anthologies *Trans Bodies, Trans Selves* (Oxford University Press) and *Writing Fire* (Green Fire Press) as well as in many journals. Lee Schwartz is two-time winner of the Allen Ginsberg Paterson Literary Prize and has served as Artist-in-Residence at the 92nd Street Y in New York City.

About Green Fire Press

Green Fire Press is an independent publishing company dedicated to supporting authors in producing and distributing high-quality books in fiction or non-fiction, poetry or prose. Find out more at Greenfirepress.com.

Other Green Fire Press titles you may also enjoy:

A Short Course In Happiness After Loss,
by Maria Sirois, PsyD

A lyrical gem of a book, combining positive psychology with the wisdom necessary to thrive when facing life's harshest moments, rising through pain into a steady, resilient and open heart.

Nature, Culture, and the Sacred: A Woman Listens For Leadership, by Nina Simons

Bioneers co-founder Nina Simons offers inspiration for anyone who aspires to grow into their own unique form of leadership with resilience and joy. Winner of the 2018 Nautilus Gold Award.

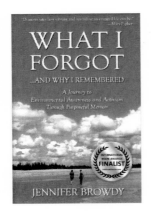

*What I Forgot…and Why
I Remembered: A Journey to
Environmental Awareness and
Activism Through Purposeful
Memoir,* by Jennifer Browdy, PhD.

"Inspires us to see how we can
reclaim our lives for the sake of life
on Earth"
—Joanna Macy.

Finalist for the 2018 International
Book Award.

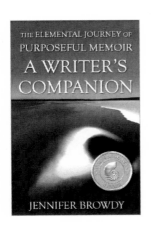

*The Elemental Journey of Purposeful
Memoir:
A Writer's Companion,*
by Jennifer Browdy, PhD

Month-by-month guidance for
memoir writers.

Winner of the 2017 Nautilus Silver
Award.

Writing Fire: Celebrating the Power of Women's Words, edited by Jennifer Browdy, Jana Laiz and Sahra Bateson Brubeck

More than 75 passionate women writers share their voices and visions in this powerful anthology.

Wisdom Lessons: Spirited Guidance from an Ojibwe Great-Grandmother, by Mary Lyons

The culmination of a lifetime steeped in Indigenous spiritual traditions, Grandmother Mary offers invaluable lessons for anyone interested in living in alignment with their higher self.

Impact with Wings: Stories to Inspire and Mobilize Women Angel Investors and Entrepreneurs, by Suzanne Andrews, Jagruti Bhikha, Karen Bairley Kruger, Christine Emilie Lim, Wingee Sin and Hana Yang With Contributing Authors Geri Stengel and Susan Preston

WILL YOU SETTLE FOR LEAVING HALF THE WORLD'S WEALTH ON THE TABLE?

In a world where women's capital remains underused, angel investing—providing money, human capital, and expertise for start-up or early-stage companies—offers a potent opportunity for women to impact the future. The authors—all seasoned players in the global business and investment community—share their personal stories and insiders' insights in a clarion wake-up call intended to activate new women angel investors.

I Give You My Word: Women's Letters as Life Support, 1973–1987, by Signe Eklund Schaefer

A forgotten box of letters in a dark attic corner, messages from women friends written decades ago. An intimate record of a time of great transition in how women experienced their daily lives and imagined their future.

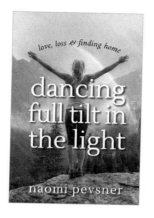

Dancing Full Tilt in the Light: Love, Loss & Finding Home, by Naomi Pevsner

A fifth generation diamond dealer whose ancestors were once diamond purveyors to the Czars of Russia, Naomi finds herself in a place so dark that even the diamonds have lost their shine. *Dancing Full Tilt In The Light* pays tribute to her journey through devastating loss to the rainbow's end of healing and home.

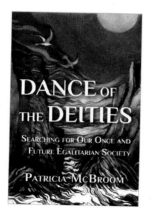

Dance of the Deities, by Patricia McBroom

Patricia McBroom compiles evidence of the ancient Nature goddesses, while calling for contemporary women to replace comic book images of feminine beauty with authentic Earth-based images of female power and authority.

Coming Soon from Green Fire Press:

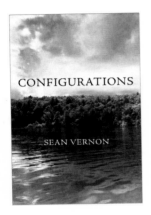

Configurations by Sean Vernon

This is Sean Vernon's first book of poems. He has published essays in periodicals such as *Smithsonian Magazine* and earned an MFA from the Writer's Workshop at the University of Iowa. He has released several albums of his musical settings for poems by William Blake, Emily Dickinson, William Butler Yeats and others. He is also co-author of a children's book, *Blanket of Stars*.

Made in United States
North Haven, CT
15 December 2021

12788725R00062